The Rockwool Foundation Research Unit

Socioeconomic status in early childhood and severe mental illness:
An empirical investigation of all Danish men born in 1981

Jane Greve

University Press of Southern Denmark
Odense 2012

**Socioeconomic status in early childhood and severe mental illness:
An empirical investigation of all Danish men born in 1981**

Study Paper No. 45

Published by:
© The Rockwool Foundation Research Unit and
University Press of Southern Denmark

Copying from this book is permitted only within
institutions that have agreements with CopyDan,
and only in accordance with the limitations laid
down in the agreement

Address:
The Rockwool Foundation Research Unit
Sølvgade 10, 2nd floor
DK-1307 Copenhagen K

Telephone   +45 33 34 48 00

Fax   +45 33 34 48 99

E-mail   forskningsenheden@rff.dk

Home page   www.rff.dk

ISBN 978-87-90199-77-7
ISSN 0908-3979
November 2012
Print run: 350
Printed by: Specialtrykkeriet Viborg

Price: 60.00 DKK, including 25% VAT

Contents

1 Introduction.. 6

2 Background.. 8

3 Methods... 10

4 Data description... 10

5 Empirical results.. 16

    5.1 The relative risk of developing schizophrenia, affective disorders and personality disorders........................... 16

    5.2 The predicted probabilities of developing schizophrenia, affective disorders and personality disorders........................... 24

6 Conclusion.. 26

References.. 27

Appendix.. 29

Socioeconomic status in early childhood and severe mental illness: An empirical investigation of all Danish men born in 1981

Jane Greve[a]*

Abstract: Mental illnesses, such as schizophrenia, affective disorders and personality disorders, are associated with heavy economic and non-economic burdens. This paper examines the relationship between socioeconomic status in early childhood and the probability of developing schizophrenia, affective disorders and personality disorders. We use a sample of all Danish men born in 1981 and control for family factors one year before the birth of the child. The results show that men born in low-income families are more likely to be hospitalized with affective disorders. Men born in families where the father was not employed at the child's birth are more likely to be hospitalized with schizophrenia or personality disorder, than men born in families where the father was employed as wage-earner.

In general, few people in the population have a severe mental illnesses and, consequently, the probability of developing a severe mental illness is low. However, the relative differences in the predicted probability of developing a mental illness are large when we compare children who grew up families with average characteristics with children who grew up in families with low socioeconomic status, i.e., household income is low, parental education is basic, and parental occupational status is not employed.

Keywords: childhood socioeconomic status, severe mental illness, Danish administrative data, cohort study
JEL codes: I10

[a] Rockwool Foundation Research Unit, Sølvgade 10, 2. tv., 1307 Copenhagen K, Denmark
* Corresponding author: tel: +45 3334 4806 fax:+45 3334 4899; email adress: jg@rff.dk

1 Introduction

The proportion of people affected worldwide by severe mental illnesses was estimated by WHO in 2001 to be approximately 10% (WHO, 2001). Although it is uncertain whether the number of people with a severe mental illness is increasing, the number of people treated at the hospital for a mental illness increased 42% from 2000 to 2008 in Denmark (Danske Regioner, 2010; Madsen et al., 2010). Studies from other countries show a similar increase in the number of people being treated for mental illness (Kessler et al., 2005). As many severe mental illnesses start to develop at an early stage (Maughan & Kim-Cohen, 2005), these illnesses impose significant social and economic burdens over lifetime. The costs related to the number of people with mental illness include both direct medical costs and a number of indirect costs due to the related morbidity and mortality (Pedersen, 2011).

Most research shows that mental illness is caused by a combination of biological, psychological and social factors (Kendler et al., 1995). This paper examines whether early childhood socioeconomic factors, i.e. family income, the parents' education and their occupational status, are related to the development of severe mental illnesses such as schizophrenia, affective disorders and personality disorders.

Previous literature has examined the association between early childhood socioeconomic factors and the development of a mental illness (Miech et al., 1999; Lahelma et al., 2006; McLaughlin et al., 2011) and seems to agree that people with mental illness are more likely to come from families with low socioeconomic status (SES), i.e., families with low household income, where the parents have few years of education and low occupational status. However, little research has examined the relative importance of the different indicators of early childhood socioeconomics factors and how they vary depending on the type of mental illness. Nor has previous research examined the importance of a combination of all risk factors, i.e., a combination of low family income, low parental education and parental non-employment.

This paper presents results on the relationship between early childhood SES factors and the development of schizophrenia, affective disorders and personality disorders. We study each of the early childhood SES factor separately and present predictions for a combination of risk factors that are likely to be associated with the development of severe mental illnesses.

Furthermore, this paper adds to the existing literature by using Danish administrative register data on psychiatric patients for all men born in Denmark in 1981 merged with register data for their parents. While previous studies (Miech et al., 1999; Lahelma et al., 2006; McLaughlin et al., 2011) measure mental illness in various ways and based on small samples of the population, the administrative register data are particularly useful in studying the relationship between early childhood factors and mental illnesses. As all Danish psychiatric hospitals are public, all admissions and discharges are recorded in the registers. Furthermore, all treatment at the psychiatric hospitals is free of charge. This means that there is no attrition rate in data and even the most severe cases of mental illnesses among the lowest SES groups are registered. Due to a unique identifier it is possible to merge information on children and parents. In particularly, information on parental education, occupation and income is registered, and included in the sample for all the years from 1980 to 2010.

Denmark makes an interesting setting to study the relationship between early childhood SES and mental illnesses. Denmark is relatively small (43,000 km^2), which means that patients have only a short distance to psychiatric hospitals, and the quality of treatment is reasonably uniform. As Denmark has a well-developed welfare system with universal health care and income security, via unemployment insurance, early retirement, etc., most cases of mental illness are at some point in time treated at a public psychiatric hospital.[1] When we base our results on the Danish administrative register data, we consequently expect to have information on almost all cases of severe mental illnesses at a given point in time.

Furthermore, Denmark with its low number of inhabitants (approx. 5 million) and a relatively dense income distribution and well-developed social security system is considered to have a relatively homogenous population. Thus, when examining the relationship between mental illnesses and childhood factors we expect to measure a lower boundary of the quantitative relationship. The significant factors revealed in this study may therefore prove to be of greater magnitude when we examine the relationship between early socioeconomic factors and mental illnesses in less homogenous countries with higher income inequality.

The results show that men born in low-income families face an increased risk of being hospitalized with affective disorders. Men born in families where the father was not employed at the child's birth are more likely to be hospitalized with schizophrenia or a personality disorder, than men born in families where the father was a wage-earner. Furthermore, the results in this paper show that a combination of risk factors related to low parental SES and social problems increase the predicted probability of developing severe mental illnesses.

The article is organized as follows. In Section 2 we provide background

---

[1] The high rate of treatment in Denmark probably explains why Denmark, in a comparative study of Denmark, the Netherlands, the UK, Italy, and Spain, has the largest costs associated with schizophrenia per patient (Andlin-Sobocki et al., 2005).

information on measures of the relevant mental illnesses and the relationship between early childhood socioeconomic factors and mental illness. In Section 3, we discusse the empirical model. In Section 4 we describe our data set and present descriptive statistics. In Section 5 we present results of the empirical analyses, and in Section 6, we discuss our results and their implications.

2 Background

In this paper we focus on the mental illnesses schizophrenia, affective disorder and personality disorder. By limiting our definition of mental illnesses to people who at some point in time have been hospitalized at a public psychiatric hospital we limit the groups of people with mental illnesses to the most severe cases. Not everybody who potentially has a diagnosable mental illness receives treatment at a public psychiatric hospital. However, by focusing on the very severe mental illnesses schizophrenia, affective disorders and personality disorders we expect to capture most of the severe cases.

We use a cohort of men born in 1981 in Denmark. Due to a personal identification number we are able to link administrative register data to a long list of variables for these men and their parents. We focus on men because men tend to develop the symptoms of many severe mental illnesses earlier than women. As we only have data up until 2010, this means that we can follow more individuals who have developed a mental illness when studying men and not women.

Several mechanisms can explain the relationship between early childhood SES and the development of a mental illness. First, many mental disorders are genetically inherited (Kendler et al., 1995) and this may cause downward mobility among adults with mental illnesses (Eaton, 1980). A transmitted illness that impairs SES may have cumulative effects through successive generations of a family, leading to a significant relationship between parental SES and the development of a severe mental illness. In our model we control for this by including a variable measuring parental mental illness.

Second, research on risk factors in the development of mental health problems has pointed to the lack of prenatal care or negative maternal life events during pregnancy such as infections and malnutrition (Gutteling et al., 2000; Xu, 2009), factors related to SES. Thus, socioeconomic differences in prenatal factors may to some extent explain the relationship between early childhood SES and the development of a severe mental illness. In the estimated models we control for this by including indicator variables for birth weight and Apgar score.

Third, parental resources, measured by household income and parental education and occupational status are important inputs during childhood in the mental health production function. The relationship between parents' education and their children's health can be understood within the framework of economic theories on health and education. In Grossman's model (1972), the relationship between education and health is explained by a more efficient health production function among parents with higher education. Alternatively, Rosenzweig and Schultz (1982) and Kenkel (1991) proposed that more schooling increases the allocative efficiency in health production, which leads to a better mix of inputs. If parents with higher education are more efficient and are better at allocating resources when producing health they will also do better in producing children's mental health. Parental education can also influence the development of mental illnesses through unobserved abilities. For example, behavior related to a good health and a good home environment have been found to be associated with longer education (Davis-Kean, 2005).

Higher household income increases possibilities of stimulating the child and buying goods needed to maintain good health throughout childhood. When we control for household income, parental occupation is a measure of differences in social status and working conditions. Parental low social status and poor working condition can affect the stress level at home in a negative way and thereby affect the development of a mental illnesses. However, there seems to be a significant variation in how children response to a risky home environment (Rutter, 2005).

While results from US shows that low parental education is associated with mental disorder persistency and severity (McLaughlin et al., 2011), a study from Finland find that low income during childhood is associated with adult psychological distress whereas parental educational attainment is not (Lahelma et al., 2006). In a study from New Zealand SES is measured as a linear composite of occupational status, educational attainment, and family income (using weights from confirmatory factor analysis) at age 15 and this measure is found to be associated with the four mental illnesses: anxiety, depression, antisocial disorder, and attention deficit disorder (Miech et al., 1999).[2]

---

[2] Lahelma et al. (2006) examines the association between childhood SES and psychological distress using the SF-36 questionnaire to identify people with common mental health problems. As we do in this paper, Miech et al. (1999) and McLaughlin et al. (2011) examine the association between early childhood SES and psychiatric outcomes. In Miech et al. (1999) the psychiatric disorders are captured in interviews using the Diagnostic Interview Schedule which generates diagnoses according to the Diagnostic and Statistical Manual of Mental Disorders (DSM) criteria. This study excludes people with schizophrenia. In McLaughlin et al. (2011) diagnoses are based on Version 3.0 of the World Health Organization Composite International Diagnostic Interview, an interview that generates diagnoses according to DSM-IV criteria.

3 Methods

We estimate three equations, one for each mental illness: schizophrenia, affective disorder and personality disorder. Let y_i be a binary variable indicating if person i has been admitted to a psychiatric hospital with one of the mental illnesses $j=s,a,p$, where s is schizophrenia, a is affective disorders and p is personality disorders. We use a logistic regression to estimate the relationship between early childhood SES and mental illness. The variables in X_i include the characteristics of the child and family, and cumulative measurements of parental health characteristics:

$$(1) \quad prob(y_{ij}) = \Lambda(X_i\beta) = \frac{\exp X_i\beta}{1+\exp X_i\beta}$$

The model is estimated on three different datasets each containing men diagnosed with the mental illnesses j, j=s,a,p, and men never diagnosed with a mental disorder. We examine the relationship between childhood SES factors on mental illness separately by diagnosis because we observe 157 men in the sample as having more than one of the three mental illnesses. As the three illnesses are all severe and some of the symptoms the same we have chosen not to assign each individual only one of the diseases and consequently estimate a model for each disease.

Many of the main control variables are correlated, e.g., father's and mother's socioeconomic characteristics. We have included all control variables stepwise to analyze to what extent the significance of the parameter estimate changes when we include other control variables. For brevity, we only include few stepwise inclusions of control variables.

Children of parents with a basic education as their highest education will often also have parents without employment and will often be born in a low-income family. We illustrate the importance of the combination of these socioeconomic factors by measuring selected predicted probabilities.

4 Data description

We construct the data by merging the Danish Psychiatric Central Register (DPCR) with various Danish administrative registers from Statistic Denmark. The DPCR contains date of all admissions, discharges, and the primary psychiatric diagnosis. This information is available for all psychiatric inpatient facilities from 1969 and all outpatient facilities from 1995 in Denmark[3]. Due to a personal identifier the

---

3 The Danish Psychiatric Central Register is described in detail in Mors, Perto & Mortensen (2011).

continuous registration of psychiatric patients in DPCR is merged with several other Danish administrative registers. We include information from the administrative register data measuring family relations, demographic and socio-demographic characteristics from 1980 and onwards in the data set. Information on hospitalization with physical illness exists from 1991 and onwards.

We select a sample of all Danish men born in 1981 and follow them until they are 29 years old in 2010. By selecting this cohort of young men we have information on their hospitalization histories up to the age of 29 together with a long list of early childhood factors related to the individual child (birth weight, Apgar score and ethnicity) and the family (family disruption, health, demographic and socio-demographic characteristics). Out of the cohort of all men born in 1981 there were 22.144 who had never been admitted to a psychiatric hospital or had an outpatient treatment and 195, 465 and 336 men who had been diagnosed with schizophrenia, affective disorders and personality disorders, respectively. This means that 9, 21 and 15 out of 1000 men have been diagnosed with schizophrenia, affective disorders and personality disorders, respectively.

With this data we are able to follow all men admitted to a psychiatric hospital in the period 1981-2010. Thus, we create a binary indicator for whether the person was admitted to a psychiatric hospital and diagnosed with one of the illnesses: schizophrenia, affective disorder and personality disorder.

Several of the related symptoms have to be observed during youth in order to be diagnosed with one of these severe mental illnesses. Thus we observe very few men with these severe mental illnesses before the age of 18. The symptoms related to schizophrenia usually develop before the age of 25 (Sham, MacLean & Kendler, 1994). For affective and personality disorders the most common age of onset is between15 and 29 (Joyce, 1984). Figure A.1 shows the cumulative admission rate from birth (year 1981) to age 29 for all the men who had ever been admitted to a psychiatric hospital with at least one of the diagnoses. The figure shows that there are very few admissions before 1994, i.e., by the age of 13. Figure A.1 also shows that in 2003, i.e. age 21, half of all cases of personality disorder had been admitted, whereas half of all the cases of affective disorder had been admitted in 2005, i.e. by the age of 23.

The mental disorders are defined on the basis of diagnoses. In our data, diagnoses are classified according to the ICD-8 system before 1994 and according to the ICD-10 system after 1994. Thus, because very few men had been admitted before 1994 the problems related to the change in the classification system do not affect the way we define the various mental illnesses.

To estimate the probability of being diagnosed with one of the mental illnesses we use three data sets that each includes all men hospitalized with the relevant mental illness and all men who had never been admitted to a psychiatric hospital. Each of the data sets therefore excludes all other men who had ever been hospitalized with a mental illness other than the relevant disorder.

The primary socioeconomic variables in this study include measurements of parental education and employment status as well as family income. See Table A1 for a detailed description of the variables. All the family socioeconomic variables are measured for the year before the child was born. For parents with missing values for the variables measuring education in 1980 we use information on education in 1981. Parental education refers to the highest completed level of education and is divided into three categories: basic education (high school or less), vocational training and further education. Parental employment status is divided into the following categories: self-employed, employed and not employed. Self-employed constitutes a separate category because self-employed people have other working conditions than employees in respect of both hours worked and income registered. Not employed people include people who receive early retirement and unemployment benefit, homemaking parents (there are very few of these), and people enrolled in education. Family income is measured as the combined gross income of both parents from all sources and calculated into quartiles.

In our models we control for a set of attributes that may influence the likelihood of developing a severe mental illness. The attributes include the following child characteristics: a binary indication for, ethnicity, region of residence at birth, high Apgar score[4] and high and low birth weight. We also include number of siblings and whether the person was the first born in the family. Being the first born in the family has some advantages, for instance a positive impact on IQ (Black, Devereux & Salvanes, 2007). Having siblings may reduce parents' time with the child, which may affect the child's development.

We also include a number of family attributes in our models to control for family environmental factors during upbringing. We use information on both the father and the mother and lag the information so parental information is derived for periods before the person was hospitalized with a mental disorder. Indicators for parental age are derived for the year the child was born. We include an indicator for teenage motherhood as children born to teenage mothers have on average more

---

4 The Apgar score is a number calculated by scoring the heart rate, respiratory effort, muscle tone, skin color, and reflex irritability. The Apgar score is recorded one and five minutes after birth and rates from 0 to 10. An Apgar score of 10 (high Apgar score) indicates that the infant is in the best possible condition. Approximately 90 % of all infants have an Apgar score of 10.

intellectual and developmental problems than children not born to teenage mothers (Brooks-Gunn & Furstenberg, 1986).

We include a list of variables indicating parental loss as this may have a significant effect on a child's psychological development. The variables measuring parental loss are measured for the years 1981 until 1996 – until the child turned 15 – and include binary indicators for the occurrence of maternal death, paternal death and parental divorce[5].

We also include a list of variables measuring parental malfunctioning as this variable can affect the child's development in general and the development of mental illnesses. We include variables for both parents indicating whether the father or the mother was hospitalized at least once in the period 1981-1996 with heart attack, stroke or cancer and whether he or she was admitted to a psychiatric hospital in the period 1969-2010. In addition we include variables indicating whether the parents had criminal records, i.e. if the father or the mother was convicted of a crime in the period 1981-1996. Parental malfunctioning may be important for the development of severe mental illness. Retrospective studies using reports of depressed adult psychiatric patients and depressed non-patients depict certain characteristics of family relationships such as less affection and tolerance and greater rejection (Coyne & Downey, 1991).

Table 1 presents descriptive statistics for the group of people with schizophrenia, affective disorders, personality disorders, and people who have never been admitted to a psychiatric hospital. We conducted standard t-tests of differences in mean values to determine whether people with mental illnesses have other characteristics than people who have never been admitted to a psychiatric hospital.

People with mental illnesses differ from people with no admission on all the early socioeconomic characteristics. In general there seems to be a relationship between mental illness and early childhood socioeconomic factors: In the groups of people with schizophrenia, affective disorders and personality disorders 41, 36 and 41 %, respectively, of the mothers are not employed when the child was born. In the group of people who have never been admitted 29 % of the mothers are not employed. The fraction of fathers without employment is 22, 15 and 25 % among people with schizophrenia, affective disorders and personality disorders, respectively. In the group of people who have never been admitted 13 % of the fathers are not employed. Among people with schizophrenia, affective disorders

---

5 We define parents as divorced when they are registered as being divorced or if they go from having the same address to not having the same address (except when this shift happens because we lose information about one of the parent's address).

and personality disorders, 30, 27 and 30 %, respectively, were born in families with an income in the lowest quartile, while among people never admitted, 18 % were born in families with an income in this quartile.

In addition, significant differences between people with a mental illness and people never admitted to a psychiatric hospital exist when we look at parental education. Among people with schizophrenia, affective disorders and personality disorders 53, 51 and 59 % of the mothers and 40, 37 and 41 % of the fathers, respectively, have a basic education as the highest completed education. Among people never admitted 45 and 31 % of the mothers and fathers, respectively, have basic education.

Below we comment on selected characteristics that differ between people with mental illnesses and people never admitted. Ten percent among people with schizophrenia and three percent among people never admitted are of another ethnicity than Danish. Among people with schizophrenia, affective disorders and personality disorders, 50, 47, and 57 %, respectively, the parents divorced before the child turned 15 years. Furthermore more people among those with mental illnesses have parents with mental health problems. Among people with schizophrenia, affective disorders and personality disorders 26, 17 and 25 % of the mothers, respectively, and 15, 14 and 17 % of the fathers, respectively, have been hospitalized with a mental illness. Among people never admitted, 8 % and 9 % of the mothers and fathers, respectively, have been hospitalized with a mental illness.

On average, people with mental illnesses have more parents with criminal records than people never admitted. However, among people with affective disorders and people never admitted, there is no significant difference in the mothers' criminal records.

Table 1 Descriptive statistics. Means for men with schizophrenia, affective disorders, personality disorders and people never admitted to psychiatric hospital. Men born in 1981.

	Schizophrenia	Affective Disorders	Personality Disorders	Never admitted to psychiatric hospital
Year 1980				
Mother, self-employed	0.021	0.019 +	0.021	0.034
Mother, employed	0.569*	0.626*	0.568*	0.676
Mother, not employed	0.41*	0.355*	0.411*	0.290
Father, self-employed	0.077	0.0538*	0.042*	0.093
Father, employed	0.703*	0.794	0.711*	0.782
Father, not employed	0.221*	0.153 +	0.247*	0.125
1st quartile	0.297*	0.269*	0.295*	0.184
2nd quartile	0.292	0.269	0.301	0.267
3rd quartile	0.19*	0.230*	0.217*	0.273
4th quartile	0.221 +	0.232*	0.188*	0.276
Year 1981				
Mother, basic education	0.528*	0.512*	0.592*	0.454
Mother, vocational	0.313	0.288 +	0.271*	0.329
Mother, further education	0.159 +	0.200	0.137*	0.217
Father, basic education	0.395*	0.368*	0.411*	0.305
Father, vocational	0.446	0.447*	0.420*	0.502
Father, further education	0.159	0.185	0.170	0.192
Low birth weight	0.036	0.052	0.066 +	0.044
High birth weight	0.031	0.024	0.015	0.023
Apgar score=10	0.954	0.940	0.923 +	0.944
Immigrant	0.103*	0.030	0.045	0.032
Urban	0.446*	0.361	0.408*	0.341
Metro	0.262	0.320	0.274	0.312
Teenage mother	0.046 +	0.043*	0.051 *	0.023
Year 1981-1996				
Parents divorced	0.503*	0.465*	0.586*	0.300
Mother, died	0.031*	0.0323*	0.027*	0.012
Father, died	0.046*	0.034 +	0.039*	0.022

	Schizophrenia	Affective Disorders	Personality Disorders	Never admitted to psychiatric hospital
Year 1991-1996				
Mother, admitted severe som.	0.021	0.015	0.009	0.016
Father, admitted severe som.	0.015	0.017	0.021*	0.018
Year 1969-2010				
Mother, admitted psych.	0.262*	0.170*	0.25*	0.083
Father, admitted psych.	0.154*	0.144*	0.167*	0.085
Year 1980-2005				
Mother, crime	0.190*	0.110	0.167*	0.102
Father, crime	0.431*	0.415*	0.47*	0.354
Year 2005				
Siblings	0.764 +	0.755*	0.732	0.706
First-born	0.554	0.548*	0.598	0.609
Number of observations	195	465	336	22,144

Note: Standard t-test of differences in means is conducted between the sample of people never admitted and each of the samples including people with mental disorders. Significance levels: .+ p<0.1, * p<0.05.

5 Empirical results

5.1 The relative risk of developing schizophrenia, affective disorders and personality disorders

Table 2, 3 and 4 show the relative risk of being hospitalized with schizophrenia, affective disorders and personality disorders, respectively. In models 1, 2 and 3 parental education, parental occupational status and family income are included separately. In model 4 all SES factors are included and in model 5 the SES factors are included together with early child characteristics (birth weight, Apgar score, immigrant status, siblings and being first born) and parental characteristics (age of parents at birth, parental divorce, parental death and parental mental and somatic illnesses).

The results in Table 2 suggest that children of father without employment at the child's birth have a higher risk of being diagnosed with schizophrenia. Odds ratio is 2.17. The correlation between the father's employment status and schizophrenia is significantly different from zero even when we control for other characteristics (model 4 and 5). In model 3, children born in families with an income in the lowest income quartile have a higher risk of being diagnosed with schizophrenia (significant at 10 %) compared to children born in the highest income quartile. However, when we control for other socio-economic factors, this odds ratio is not significantly different from zero (model 4 and 5).

Table 3 shows the relationship between socioeconomic factors in childhood and affective disorders. The results in model 1, 4 and 5 show that parental education is not associated with affective disorders. If the father was self-employed at the child's birth, the risk of being diagnosed with an affective disorder is lower than if the father was wage-earner. The odds ratio is 0.55. Children born in families with incomes in the lowest income quartile have a higher risk of being diagnosed with affective disorders compared to children who are born in the highest income quartile. The odds ratio is approximately 1.6.

Men with a mother with a basic education have a higher risk of being diagnosed with personality disorders than men with a mother with a further education. However, Table 4, model 4, shows that this odds ratio is not significant different from zero when we control for other socioeconomic characteristics. The relationship between mothers' occupational status and the development of personality disorders is also insignificant when we include other controls. If the father was not employed at the child's birth, the risk of developing personality disorder is higher than if the father was wage-earner. Odds ratio is 2.24, but is reduced to 2.0, when we control for other socio-economic factors (model 4), and to 1.7, when we control for other child and parental characteristics (model 5). If the father was self-employed the risk of developing a personality disorders is lower than if the father was wage-earner. Family income at the child's birth shows a significant correlation with the development of personality disorders in model 3, but this correlation is not significant different form zero when we include other controls in the model (model 4 and 5).

Several of the child and parental characteristics we include in model 5 are significant risk factors for developing mental illnesses. The developments of all three mental illnesses are associated with parental mental health. If the mother was admitted to a psychiatric hospital before the child turned 15 years old the child is more likely to develop schizophrenia, affective disorder and personality disorder (the odds ratios are 2.7, 1,5 and 2.4, respectively). If the father was admitted to a psychiatric hospital the child is also more likely to develop of schizophrenia and affective disorders (the odds ratios are 1.6 and 1.5, respectively). To be diagnosed with affective disorders and personality disorders is associated with parental divorce, before the child turned 15. The odds ratio is 1.5 for affective disorders and 2.2 for personality disorders. Immigrants and people living in an urban area rather than a rural area have higher risk of developing schizophrenia. The first born children in the family have lower odds of developing an affective disorder.

Table 2 Associations between childhood socioeconomic factors and schizophrenia. Logistic regression – odds ratio – for being admitted to a psychiatric hospital with schizophrenia. Confidence interval in brackets.

	Model 1	Model 2	Model 3	Model 4	Model 5
Mother, basic education	1.27			1.12	0.97
	[0.70;2.29]			[0.60;2.07]	[0.52;1.81]
Mother, vocational education	1.38			1.36	1.30
	[0.76;2.49]			[0.75;2.47]	[0.71;2.37]
Father, basic education	1.52			1.26	1.12
	[0.80;2.88]			[0.65;2.45]	[0.57;2.19]
Father, vocational education	1.26			1.16	1.20
	[0.69;2.30]			[0.63;2.13]	[0.65;2.21]
Mother, unemployed		1.29		1.20	1.05
		[0.87;1.91]		[0.78;1.84]	[0.68;1.62]
Mother, self-employed		0.24		0.23	0.24
		[0.03;1.83]		[0.03;1.74]	[0.03;1.81]
Father, unemployed		2.17***		2.05**	1.66*
		[1.38;3.41]		[1.27;3.29]	[1.01;2.71]
Father, self-employed		1.58		1.56	1.71
		[0.83;3.03]		[0.81;3.01]	[0.88;3.33]
1st quartile			1.70+	1.17	0.94
			[0.97;2.97]	[0.63;2.20]	[0.49;1.80]
2nd quartile			1.50	1.23	1.23
			[0.88;2.55]	[0.70;2.16]	[0.69;2.18]
3rd quartile			1.13	1.02	1.11
			[0.65;1.99]	[0.57;1.82]	[0.62;1.98]
Low birth weight					0.54
					[0.17;1.73]
High birth weight					1.34
					[0.42;4.25]
Apgar score = 10					1.25
					[0.50;3.09]

Empirical results

	Model 1	Model 2	Model 3	Model 4	Model 5
Immigrant					3.38***
					[1.78;6.41]
Siblings					1.28
					[0.77;2.12]
Firstborn					0.93
					[0.59;1.45]
Teenage mother					1.08
					[0.41;2.85]
Parents divorced					1.26
					[0.82;1.91]
Father, died					1.52
					[0.58;3.94]
Mother, admitted psych.					2.67***
					[1.68;4.23]
Father, admitted psych.					1.63 +
					[0.96;2.77]
Mother, crime					1.50
					[0.91;2.46]
Father, crime					1.22
					[0.81;1.82]
Mother, admitted severe som.					0.87
					[0.12;6.27]
Father, admitted severe som.					0.84
					[0.20;3.57]
Urban					1.58 +
					[0.97;2.59]
Metro					1.21
					[0.72;2.03]
Observations	23,532	23,532	23,532	23,532	23,532

Level of significance: + p<0,1, * p<0,05, ** p<0,01, *** p<0,001

Table 3 Associations between childhood socioeconomic factors and affective disorder. Logistic regression – odds ratio – for being admitted to a psychiatric hospital with an affective disorder. Confidence interval in brackets.

	Model 1	Model 2	Model 3	Model 4	Model 5
Mother, basic education	0.96			0.89	0.82
	[0.70;1.30]			[0.64;1.22]	[0.59;1.13]
Mother, vocational education	0.84			0.81	0.80
	[0.61;1.15]			[0.59;1.12]	[0.58;1.11]
Father, basic education	1.23			1.19	1.12
	[0.87;1.73]			[0.84;1.70]	[0.78;1.61]
Father, vocational education	1.01			1.02	1.01
	[0.73;1.39]			[0.74;1.41]	[0.73;1.40]
Mother, unemployed		1.13		0.99	0.95
		[0.90;1.43]		[0.76;1.27]	[0.73;1.23]
Mother, self-employed		0.90		0.88	0.87
		[0.40;1.99]		[0.39;1.94]	[0.39;1.95]
Father, unemployed		1.07		0.92	0.85
		[0.78;1.46]		[0.66;1.27]	[0.61;1.17]
Father, self-employed		0.55*		0.53*	0.52
		[0.33;0.92]		[0.31;0.89]	[0.31;0.88]
1st quartile			1.60**	1.59**	1.53*
			[1.17;2.18]	[1.12;2.25]	[1.07;2.19]
2nd quartile			1.23	1.21	1.20
			[0.91;1.66]	[0.87;1.66]	[0.87;1.66]
3rd quartile			1.04	1.01	1.04
			[0.76;1.42]	[0.73;1.40]	[0.75;1.44]
Low birth weight					1.00
					[0.61;1.65]
Heigh birth weight					0.79
					[0.35;1.78]

	Model 1	Model 2	Model 3	Model 4	Model 5
Apgar score = 10					1.04
					[0.65;1.67]
Immigrant					0.52
					[0.22;1.19]
Siblings					1.01
					[0.75;1.35]
Firstborn					0.75*
					[0.58;0.98]
Teenage mother					1.22
					[0.69;2.14]
Parents divorced					1.48**
					[1.16;1.88]
Father, died					1.08
					[0.57;2.03]
Mother, died					1.97 +
					[0.97;4.00]
Mother, admitted psych.					1.54**
					[1.13;2.09]
Father, admitted psych.					1.54**
					[1.12;2.13]
Mother, crime					0.70 +
					[0.48;1.02]
Father, crime					1.17
					[0.93;1.47]
Mother, admitted severe som.					0.92
					[0.39;2.16]
Father, admitted severe som.					1.04
					[0.48;2.24]
Urban					0.96
					[0.73;1.26]
Metro					1.04
					[0.80;1.36]
Observations	23,761	23,761	23,761	23,761	23,761

Level of significance: + p<0,1, * p<0,05, ** p<0,01, *** p<0,001

Table 4 Associations between childhood socioeconomic factors and personality disorder. Logistic regression – odds ratio – for being admitted to a psychiatric hospital with a personality disorder. Confidence interval in brackets.

	Model 1	Model 2	Model 3	Model 4	Model 5
Mother, basic education	1.83**			1.457	1.255
	[1.18;2.82]			[0.93;2.29]	[0.79;1.99]
Mother, vocational education	1.32			1.222	1.186
	[0.84;2.07]			[0.77;1.93]	[0.75;1.88]
Father, basic education	1.18			0.977	0.847
	[0.77;1.81]			[0.63;1.52]	[0.54;1.33]
Father, vocational education	0.79			0.751	0.720
	[0.53;1.20]			[0.49;1.14]	[0.47;1.10]
Mother, unemployed		1.56**		1.310+	1.211
		[1.18;2.05]		[0.97;1.77]	[0.89;1.64]
Mother, self-employed		0.86		0.800	0.861
		[0.26;2.81]		[0.24;2.64]	[0.26;2.84]
Father, unemployed		2.24***		2.002***	1.698**
		[1.65;3.03]		[1.45;2.77]	[1.22;2.36]
Father, self-employed		0.36*		0.364*	0.389*
		[0.15;0.83]		[0.16;0.85]	[0.17;0.91]
1st quartile			2.251***	1.347	1.178
			[1.49;3.39]	[0.85;2.14]	[0.73;1.90]
2nd quartile			1.899**	1.424	1.385
			[1.28;2.82]	[0.93;2.17]	[0.90;2.12]
3rd quartile			1.345	1.146	1.193
			[0.88;2.05]	[0.74;1.77]	[0.77;1.85]
Low birth weight					1.24
					[0.73;2.10]
Heigh birth weight					0.71
					[0.23;2.25]
Apgar score = 10					0.71
					[0.44;1.15]

	Model 1	Model 2	Model 3	Model 4	Model 5
Immigrant					0.91
					[0.45;1.83]
Siblings					1.06
					[0.75;1.48]
Firstborn					1.06
					[0.77;1.48]
Teenage mother					0.81
					[0.41;1.61]
Parents divorced					2.21***
					[1.63;2.98]
Father, died					1.09
					[0.56;2.14]
Mother, died					0.89
					[0.28;2.89]
Mother, admitted psych.					2.42***
					[1.75;3.34]
Father, admitted psych.					1.36
					[0.93;1.97]
Mother, crime					0.97
					[0.66;1.42]
Father, crime					1.25
					[0.94;1.67]
Mother, admitted severe som.					0.31
					[0.04;2.27]
Father, admitted severe som.					1.61
					[0.74;3.55]
Urban					0.97
					[0.70;1.35]
Metro					0.76
					[0.54;1.07]
Observations	23,641	23,641	23,641	23,641	23,641

Level of significance: + p<0,1, * p<0,05, ** p<0,01, *** p<0,001

5.2 The predicted probabilities of developing schizophrenia, affective disorders and personality disorders

Table 3 presents the predicted probabilities of developing schizophrenia, affective disorder and personality disorder. These probabilities show the absolute risk of developing a mental illness for people with specific characteristics and are, in general, small. In the first row of Table 3 we have calculated the predicted probability of being hospitalized with schizophrenia (column 1), affective disorder (column 2) and personality disorder (column 3) for a baseline person. The characteristics for the baseline person are: normal birth weight, high APGAR score, ethnic Danish, having siblings, being firstborn, mother was not a teenager when the child was born, parents living together, neither parent having been hospitalized with mental illness, neither parent having a criminal record, neither parent having a hospital record, the child living in Copenhagen area when born, both parents having a vocational education, both parents being wage-earners, family income in the 2nd quartile. For a person with the baseline characteristics the probability of being diagnosed with schizophrenia is 0.4%, with affective disorder is 0.8%, and with personality disorder is 0.4%.

Often parents in the lowest income quartile will also be without work and without a further education. We have therefore calculated the predicted probability of developing schizophrenia, affective disorders and personality disorders for people who have a combination of the factors measuring high and low socio-economic status (SES) in childhood. In addition, we have estimated the predicted probability of developing one of the mental illnesses for men who grew up in families with low SES and where either the parents are divorced, the father is registered for crime or the parents had been hospitalized with a mental illness.

The results in Table 5 show that the predicted probability of developing schizophrenia for men who grew up in families with high SES, i.e., the parents have a further education, are employed wage-earners and have an income in the highest quartile, is 0.2 %. This predicted probability is considerably less than for a baseline person. There are only minor differences in predicted probability of developing affective disorders and personality disorders for men growing up in a family with high SES and men who grew up in an average (baseline) family. The predicted probabilities of developing affective disorders and personality disorders, for men who grew up in a high SES family, is 0.99 % and 0.4 %, respectively.

The predicted probabilities of developing schizophrenia, affective disorder or personality disorder for men who grew in a low SES family is 0.4 %, 1.1 %, and 1.1 %, respectively. Thus, there are significant (relative) differences in the probability of being diagnosed with affective disorders and personality disorders for men growing up in a low SES family and men growing up in an average family. The predicted probability of developing schizophrenia is almost the same for a man with average characteristics (a baseline person) and a man growing up in a low SES family.

The predicted probabilities of developing severe mental illnesses increase significantly when men, growing up in low SES families, have other indicators of social problems. The results in Table 5 show that the predicted probabilities for men growing up in a low SES family, where the parents are divorced and the father has a criminal record, are 0.7 %, 2.3 %, and 2.3 % for schizophrenia, affective disorders and personality disorders. This means that the predicted probabilities are 2 (schizophrenia), 3 (affective disorders) and 6 (personality disorders) times higher for men in this fragile group than they are for a baseline person.

The combination of growing up in a low SES family and having either mother or a father who have been hospitalized with a mental illness also increases the predicted probabilities of developing a mental illness significantly compared to men growing up in a family with baseline characteristics.

Table 5 Predicted probability of being admitted to a psychiatric hospital with schizophrenia, affective disorders, and personality disorders. Sample includes all men born in 1981, living in Denmark.

	Schizophrenia	Affective disorder	Personality disorder
Baseline person[1]	0.0042	0.0084	0.0042
High SES[2]	0.0025	0.0099	0.0042
Low SES[3]	0.0043	0.0112	0.0107
Low SES and parents divorced	0.0054	0.0164	0.0232
Low SES, parents divorced and father has a criminal record	0.0071	0.0231	0.0236
Low SES and the father has been admitted to a psychiatric hospital	0.0070	0.0171	0.0144
Low SES and the mother has been admitted to a psychiatric hospital	0.0112	0.0170	0.0254

Notes: [1] Baseline categories are: normal birth weight, high Apgar-score, Danish ethnicity, has siblings, is the first born, mother was not teenage mother, parents live together, parents are not dead, none of the parents have been admitted to a psychiatric hospital, none of the parents have been hospitalized at a somatic hospital with severe somatic diseases, none of the parents are registered for crime, parents lived in the area of Copenhagen at the child's birth, both parents have a vocational education, both parents are wage-earners, family income is 3rd quartile.
[2] The categories for high SES are the same as the baseline categories but both parents have a further education and family income is in the 4th quartile.
[3] The categories for low SES are the same as the baseline categories but both parents have a basic education, both parents are not employed and family income is in the 1st quartile.

6 Conclusion

Mental illnesses such as schizophrenia, affective disorders and personality disorders are severe and burdensome illnesses. Prospective longitudinal research has shown that a substantial continuity of these diseases through a lifetime means impaired functioning in work and in social and family life. Mental illnesses tend to develop early in life and early symptoms of these illnesses may affect educational decisions and outcomes as well as the individual's economic situation later in life. Consequently, it is important to distinguish between socioeconomic status (SES) early in life and the development of severe mental illnesses later in life and to analyze which, and to what extent, early SES can be protective against the development of severe mental illnesses.

This paper contributes to the literature by using Danish administrative register data on psychiatric patients for all men born in Denmark in 1981 merged with register data for their parents. As all Danish psychiatric hospitals are public, all admissions and discharges are recorded in the registers. Accordingly, we have no attrition in our data and the analysis includes all people – also the most severe cases and those born in families with the lowest SES – with one of the relevant disorders. Furthermore, information from the administrative register data from 1980 and onwards provides precise information on both very early childhood characteristics, such as birth weight and Apgar score, and parental SES a year before the child's birth, which reduces concerns about reverse causality.

Our findings suggest that the SES of the family during early childhood is significantly related to the development of severe mental illnesses. In particular, we find that men, whose father was not employed at the child's birth, have a higher risk of being diagnosed with schizophrenia or personality disorder than men whose father was wage-earners. Men growing up in low income households (in the 1st quartile) have a higher average risk of being diagnosed with affective disorder. However, this relationship is not necessarily causal. If certain unobserved charcteristics are corirelated with both the risk of developing an affective disorder and being from a lowincome family, these unobserved charcteristics may explain the relationship between low income and the probability af developing an affective disorder. We do not find an association between parental education and the development of a mental disorder. The differences in the significance of the SES factors depending on the diagnosis may explain why previous literature has not been able to point to a single SES as the most important.

We have calculated the absolute risk of developing a severe mental illness. Although the probabilities of developing schizophrenia, affective disorder and personality disorders are very small, there are significant relative differences in the probabilities depending on the combination of the parental characteristics before the child's birth. We find that the predicted probabilities of developing severe mental illnesses increase significantly when men growing up in low SES families have other indicators of social problems.

The socioeconomic factors analyzed here, i.e., low parental income, educational and occupational categories cannot be interpreted as causal factors. However, the identification of a combination of risk factors and the differences depending on the diagnosis indicates that there are vulnerable groups among low SES families where the risk of developing a severe mental illness is higher.

References

Andlin-Sobocki, P., Jönsson, B., Wittchen, H., & Olesen, J. (2005). Cost of disorders of the brain in Europe, *European Journal of Neurology*, 12(Suppl. s1), 1–27.

Black, S., Devereux, P., & Salvanes, K. (2007). Older and Wiser? Birth Order and IQ of Young Men. *NBER Working Paper*, no. 13237.

Brooks-Gunn, J., & Furstenberg, F.F. (1986). The children of adolescent mothers: Physical, academic and psychological outcomes. *Developmental Review*, 6, 224-251.

Coyne, J.C., & Downey, G. (1991). Social factors and psychopathology: stress, social support, and coping processes. *Annual Review of Psychology*, 42, 401-425.

Danske Regioner (2010). Benchmarking af psykiatrien – herunder nøgletal for aktiviteten i 2009, *Danske Regioner, København*.

Davis-Kean, P. (2005). The Influence of Parent Education and Family Income on Child Achievement: The Indirect Role of Parental Expectations and the Home Environment. *Journal of Family Psychology*, 19(2), 294–304.

Gutteling, B. M., de Weerth, C., Willemsen-Swinkels, S. H. N., Huizink, Huizink, A.C., Mulder, E. J. H., Visser, G. H. A., & Buitelaar, J. K. (2005). The effects of prenatal stress on temperament and problem behavior of 27-month-old toddlers. *European Child & Adolescent Psychiatry*, 14(1), 41-51.

Joyce, PR. (1984). Age of onset in bipolar affective disorder and misdiagnosis as schizophrenia. *Psychological Medicine: A Journal of Research in Psychiatry and the Allied Sciences*, 14(1), 145-149.

Kendler, K.S. (1995). Genetic epidemiology in psychiatry. Taking both genes and environment seriously. *Archives of General Psychiatry*, 52(11), 895-899.

Kenkel, D. S. (1991). Health Behavior, Health Knowledge, and Schooling. *Journal of Political Economy*, 99(2), 287-305. University of Chicago Press.

Kessler, et al., (2005). Prevalence and Treatment of Mental Disorders, 1990 to 2003. *The New England Journal of* Medicine, 352, 2515-2523.

Lahelma, E., Laaksonen, M., Martikainen, P., Rahkonen, O., & Sarlio-Lähteenkorva, S. (2006). Multiple measures of socioeconomic circumstance and common mental disorders. *Social Science & Medicine*, 63(5), 1383-1399.

Madsen, M., Hvenegaard, A., & Fredslund E. (2010). Opgaveudvikling på psykiatriområdet. Opgaver og udfordringer i kommunerne i relation til borgere med psykiske problemstillinger. Dansk Sundhedsinstitut, København.

Maughan, B. & Kim-Cohen, J. (2005). Continuities between childhood and adult life. *British Journal of Psychiatry*, 187, 301-303.

McLaughlin, K., Breslau, J., Green, J. G., Lakoma, M. D., Sampson, N. A., Zaslavsky, A. M., & Kessler, R. C. (2011). Childhood socio-economic status and the onset, persistence, and severity of DSM-IV mental disorders in a US national sample. *Social Science & Medicine*, 73(7), 1088-1096.

Miech, R. A., Caspi, A., Moffitt, T. E., Wright, B. R. E., & Silva, P. A. (1999). Low Socioeconomic Status and Mental Disorders: A Longitudinal Study of Selection and Causation during Young Adulthood. *American Journal of Sociology*, 104(4), 1096-1131. The University of Chicago Press.

Mors, O., Perto, G. P., & Mortensen, P. B. (2011). The Danish Psychiatric Central Research Register. *Scandinavian Journal of Public Health*, 39(7), 54–57.

Rutter, M. (2005). How the environment affects mental health. *British Journal of Psychiatry.* 186, 4-6.

Sham, P. C., MacLean C.J., & Kendler, K. S. (1994). A typological model of schizophrenia based on age at onset, sex and familial morbidity. *Acta Psychiatrica Scandinavica.* 89(2), 135-141.

WHO (2001) *The World Health Report 2001 – Mental Health: New Understanding, New Hope.* World Health Organization Geneva.

Xu, M., Sun, W., Liu, B., Feng, G., Yu, L., Yang, L., He, G., Sham, P., Susser, E., St. Clair, D., & He, L. (2009). Prenatal Malnutrition and Adult Schizophrenia: Further Evidence From the 1959-1961 Chinese Famine. *Schizophrenia Bulletin*, 35(3), 568-576.

Appendix

Figure A.1 Year at first admission among men born in 1981.

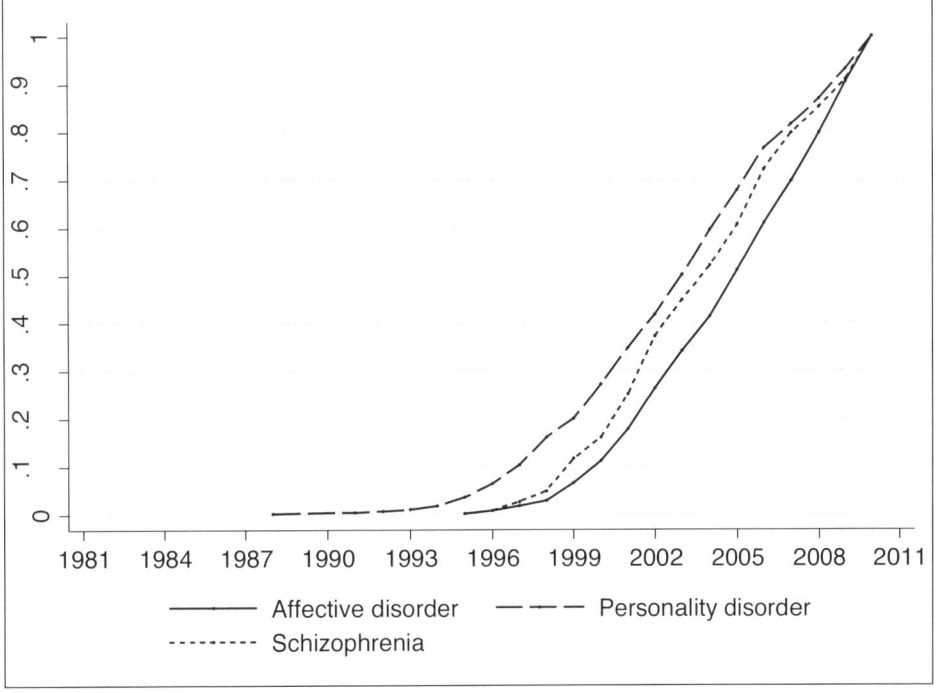

Table A1 Detailed description of variables from administrative registerdata 1969-2010.

Dependent variable, mental illness among men born in 1981
Schizophrenia: (0/1) 1 if hospitalized with schizophrenia (ICD-8 codes: 29,509-29,599 and ICD-10 code: F20) in the period 1981-2010
Affective disorder: (0/1) 1 if hospitalized with affective disorder (ICD-8 codes: 29,609-29,699 and ICD-10 codes: F30-39) in the period 1981-2010
Personality disorder: (0/1) 1 if hospitalized with ′personality disorder (ICD-8 codes: 30,109-30,199 and ICD-10 codes: F60-69) in the period 1981-2010:

Early socioeconomic variables
Education in 1981: one variable for father and one variable for mother
Mother/Father basic education: (0/1) 1 if mother's/father's education is basic schooling
Mother/Father vocational: (0/1) 1 if mother's/father's education is vocational training or high school
Mother/Father further education: (0/1) 1 if mother's/father's education is further ????

Occupation in 1980: one variable for father and one variable for mother
Mother/Father not employed: (0/1) 1 if unemployed or out of the labor market
Mother/Father self-employed: (0/1)
Mother/Father employed: (0/1) 1 if wage earner

Household income in 1980: Sum of father's and mother's gross income in quartiles
1st quartile: (0/1) 1 if the sum of father's and mother's gross income in the first quartile in the income distribution for the whole population in 1980
2nd quartile: (0/1) 1 if income between 117,945 and 157,790 DKK
3rd quartile: (0/1) 1 if income between 157,792 and 188,727 DKK
4th quartile: (0/1) 1 if income above 188,729 and 4,502,219 DKK

Child variables, all measured in 1981
Birth weight (BW):
Low birth weight: (0/1) 1 if BW<2500
Heigh birth weight: (0/1) 1 if BW>4500

Apgar score: (0/1) 1 if Apgar score =10

Immigrant: (0/1) 1 if not ethnic Dane

Siblings: (0/1) 1 if having one or more siblings

Firstborn: (0/1) 1 if being the mother's firstborn

Family variables
Metropol: (0/1) 1 if living in metropolitan area
Urban: (0/1) 1 if living in urban area
Rural: (0/1) 1 if living in rural area

Teenage mother: mother below 20 at child's birth

Parental loss
Parents divorced, 1981-1996: 1 if parents are registered as being divorced or if they go from having the same address to not having the same address, except when this shift happens because we lose information about one of the parent's address.
Father died, 1981-1996: 1 if dead

Parental absence and malfunctioning
Admitted to a hospital with a severe physical disease, 1991-1996 : one variable for father and one variable for mother
Mother/father admitted: (0/1) 1 if mother/father was admitted with heart attack or angina pectoris, stroke or cerebral hemorrhage, or cancer in the years 1991-1996

Admitted to a psychiatric hospital, 1969-2010: one variable for father and one variable for mother
Mother/father admitted: (0/1) 1 if mother/father was admitted to a psychiatric hospital in the years 1969-2010

Crime 1980-1996:
Mother/father crime: (0/1) 1 if mother/father has been convicted of crime in the years 1980-1996